RASTAFARI?
RASTA FOR YOU
Rastafarianism Explained

Contents

Introduction

Jamaica is so small, small for us, but as the older folks say (my ancestors) 'Lilly, but *mi tallawah*.' Small, but we are known nearly everywhere. But yet, when we are in Jamaica, we think about other countries even though we are not well known in other parts of the world. Like many young Jamaicans, I've never travelled a lot apart from within Jamaica. Maybe while I was in Jamaica, if someone asked me, 'Do you like to travel?' or, 'Which countries would you like to visit?' I would have said the United States, England, or somewhere small where people speak English. Since my childhood years I've heard adults say this. They thought that visiting other countries, apart from ones that spoke English, would be difficult; they would feel so alienated – no way!

Just before my adulthood, I had an opportunity to visit Europe. I call this an opportunity, because it was not only to visit Europe but also to visit France. Now my dream has been realised because I've always wanted to visit another country where they speak another language apart from mine, or Spanish. My decision was quickly made – es! I was excited; I didn't even think of how it would be for me in another country that I knew nothing about – and I don't even understand a word of French. The only thing I knew was that I had a friend living there. So I thought, maybe he can help me to understand a little bit of French.

Upon reaching France, while I was in the airport, I listened to how they spoke; I started trying to see if I could understand, but I couldn't understood a word. Now I started feeling alienated, and wondered about how it would be for me. After a few months, I started feeling the need to learn this language. I made a promise to learn French with all my heart and mind. I began trying to find information on how or where I could learn it. After a few months of research, I finally found a place that accepted me. Finally I started learning French in a high school where they had a class for foreigners.

I was the only one of English-speaking origin, so it was very difficult for me to communicate with others, even with my dictionary. Each day at school was more and more difficult for me. Almost all the students were women, with the exception of one male. The first day at school, we all introduced ourselves. When it was my turn to speak everyone started laughing when they heard my accent. But this really didn't bother me. I never understood anything; while the women introduced themselves, the only thing I understood were their names. After three weeks at school, the teacher was amazed by my progress. By communicating with the women, I started losing confidence in myself, because most of these women had been learning French for approximately five to ten years. Anyway, I decided, if I really wanted to speak this language I could. The more time passed the more my knowledge and vocabulary grew.

'At the end of the month, there will be an exam,' said the teacher one day. 'This exam determines who will stay in the same class and who will progress to a more advanced class.' She continued. 'This class is called "alba", which means that this is the first stage of the learning process. After which is "déclin" for those who can read and write in French.'

Most of these women had never been to school – they did not even know how to comport themselves in public. Most of the time, they spoke in their language that was mostly Arabic. When the teacher asked them why they didn't speak French, they just smiled. After that, I came to the conclusion that there was no secret to learning a language; if someone tries to learn a new language and always speaks in their mother tongue, they will never learn the new language. After six months of study, I thought I was now capable of understanding if someone asked me a question.

At the same time, I was curious to know many things. I even started comparing certain things with those in Jamaica. Everything was different; the language, of course; their expressions; the food, and most of all, the climate. Not only when it's winter, it surprises me, but during summer, the sunshine that I've seen nearly every day in Jamaica – that I call very hot – here, I have the impression that it's two times hotter than in Jamaica!

When it's spring, the country amazes me; many places are so beautiful, the trees awake and there are lots of beautiful flowers on the ground. With all the experiences I've had here, I would like to know what the French think of Jamaica. Jamaica is not well known by the French. As for the Jamaicans, France is not well known. The French learn of Jamaica through the media or through Jamaican music. By listening to their point of view, I concluded that, for most of them, Jamaica is an island with many Rastas who use cannabis. And there are lots of smokers, there are marijuana plants in abundance, and if you want these experiences, the place to visit is Jamaica. They also talk about reggae music; and for them, Bob Marley is a legend that lives on. In addition, 'Rastas', for them, are Peter Tosh, Toots and the Maytals, Burning Spear and the group Israel Vibration, because these are the few internationally famed Jamaican artists that they know or maybe heard about. They know that these artists have the joy of living just by listening to their music.

I explained to them that Jamaica was not like that. I even told them that if they ever visited Jamaica it would not meet up to their expectations. They should not believe the media or someone who went there on holiday only for one week. In one week, they won't discover anything. And cannabis is strictly prohibited there. The film called *The Harder They Come* with Jimmy Cliff also influences them. They think Jamaican life is really like that, but now I explain things and times have also changed. Maybe in the late Seventies and early Eighties, before the prohibition, it was like they imagined; but now we are in the 21st century, and time has changed things. That's the reason why I have decided to explain the lives of Rastas in Jamaica.

Some things explained...

TRANSLATIONS

backbiters	criticism
gargamel	very attractive
ital	untreated food which generally means it contains no additives, salt or chemicals
Jah	God; Jehovah
jam down	Jamaica
mi talawah	famous, well known
skylarkers	a person who is unemployed and refuses to work

WHEN, WHERE AND HOW RASTAFARIANISM CAME ABOUT

Rastafarianism has its roots in Jamaica in the 1930s, with the prophecy of a black being crowned in Africa. The Rastas argue that, according to the bible (Psalm 87:4), there is a prophetic reference to Haile Selassie, born in Ethiopia, as being the messiah.

In the early 1920s, Garvey was an influential black spokesman and founder of the Back-to-Africa Movement. He often spoke of the redemption of his people lying in this future black African king. A few years later, the prediction was fulfilled in Ethiopia. Haile Selassie was crowned on November 2, 1930.

Upon his coronation, he claimed the title of 'Emperor Haile Selassie I' (Power of the Trinity) for himself, conquering the tribe of Judah, and elect of God and king of kings of Ethiopia.

After his crowning, the Rastafari movement gained a following and officially began in 1930. An important historical event in the Rastafari movement occurred when Haile Selassie visited Jamaica on April 21, 1966. This event results in two profound developments within the movement. First, Selassie convinced the Rastafarian brothers that they should not speak of immigrating to Ethiopia until they have liberated the people of Jamaica. Second,

11

April 21 has since been celebrated as a holy day among the Rastafarian communities, as well as August 27, the day of Haile Selassie's death.

SELASSIE I

Lij Tafari, later known as Rasta Tafari and also as Haile Selassie, was born on July 23, 1892, in Harror, Ethiopia. Before his birth, chaplains and astrologers had been foretelling the infant's birth. The planets Neptune and Pluto had started moving slowly towards each other in 1399 along the heliocentric line, taking 493 years to intersect. At this precise time, Lij Tafari was born. This was the first day of the zodiac sign, Leo, an event that would later help to prove his title at his coronation – the conquering lion of the tribe of Judah.

Lij Tafari was also the last Ethiopian emperor. He came from a strict Ethiopian orthodox family. As per the tradition, he was baptised on the fortieth day of his life. It is rumoured that as a child, he was able to speak to animals. Legend has it that he could converse with leopards and lions and these ferocious beasts would become gentle and peaceful in his presence. This is why in Jamaica today, the lion is seen as a bringer of luck to households and thus painted onto the walls of many houses.

At the age of twenty-four, Tafari was made Chief Advisor and heir to the throne of Ethiopia. With his power, he reorganised his country by building more schools and hospitals and sending Ethiopians abroad to study and uniting various regions of the nation. In 1923, he successfully interred an Ethiopian into the League of Nations, making it the first African nation to enter the League. He also established the Ethiopian society's commercial industry. He thus had a huge impact on Ethiopia and the black populations around the world.

To the Jamaican Rastas, he is a father figure, a teacher and a guide. They believe that Tafari brought them to Jamaica from Ethiopia and that he allowed them to become free – free to govern themselves. The memory of Tafari continues to live through Rastafarianism.

Rastafarianism

Rastas in Jamaica makes up about half a million out of the total population. The Rastas are called by many names; Bongo Man, Dread, Natty Bongo, Congo Man, Binghy Man, Nyiah Binghy... But the most used term is 'Rasta'.

The religion of Rastafarianism operates differently from other religions. They believe in one supreme God, which for them is Jah. They believe in unity. What they are doing is trying to capture the attention of Jamaicans to educate them about the world in which they live, which they describe as corrupt. They have their churches; they sing their songs, they pray to their supreme God, Jah, for guidance.

The Appearance of Rastas

The Rastas dress in bright-coloured clothes, with a dominance of red, green and gold. This represents Africa. They wear this like a uniform, to symbolise that they always have Africa and Jah with them, not only in their appearance, but also in their hearts.

Most Rastas' houses are decorated with bright colours also: black, red, green and gold. The black represents the people of Africa. For them, they are the people of Africa, and Jah is always with them, to show them the way, 'the right way'. On their houses, they draw a big lion, and they make a lion pendant to put on their chains, to have this iconic animal's spirit with them all the time. This lion is the conquering lion from the tribe of Judah, which protects them from their enemies, to give them faith, and to remind them not to be afraid.

The Consciousness of Rastas

The Rastas are very conscious of their black history. They think that without the existence of Rastafarians, black people in general would not be conscious of their history. They believe that Haile Selassie is the reincarnation of Christ. They also believe that without the existence of Rastas, the blacks would never receive justice in countries that are predominantly white. Eight out of ten Rastas' dream is to return to Africa – as they always say, 'Africa is our homeland, and we should settle there.'

They also believe that the black people suffer a lot of propaganda from certain white races. These Rastas seek the help of many Jamaicans, to educate them about the past and the world in which they now live. Still, certain Jamaicans reject them, because they believe these Rastas to be too strange in their thinking. Most Jamaicans would say that they don't understand the behaviour of Rastas. But Rastas believe that without behaving this way, people wouldn't understand what they meant. They even explain to people not to be surprised by theirs outfits; it's just a symbol of unity.

The Beliefs, Rituals and Symbols of Rastas

For the Rastafarians, native herbalists used ganja as a folk medicine, particularly in teas, cakes, medication and a smoking mixture with tobacco. But it now takes on a new role as a religious sacrament. They believe that not even half of the full potential of this plant has been discovered. And Western society misconstrues its use as being reactionary. The Rastas think that ganja is the only plant in history that has always been criticised by people who know nothing about it. King Solomon, who is considered to be one of the wisest men, is thought to have used this plant, because it grew near his grave. He has never revealed any of the secrets of this plant. Maybe he kept all these secrets to be wiser than everyone. And perhaps that's why the whole of Babylon is against it.

After lots of studies on marijuana, they came to the conclusion that it is the only plant that produces a psycho-spiritual effect and has medicinal functions for people suffering from stress. It produces visions and a feeling of togetherness. It dispels gloom and fear, and brings tranquillity to the minds of the so-disposed. According to Peter Tosh, in his song, 'Legalise it', it's also good for cancer, tuberculosis, asthma, just to name a few. Because this plant has such health benefits, the Rastas wait for its legalisation.

The Rastas also have particularities in their eating habits, which includes lots of vegetables, and never any red meat. But they do eat lots of fish, which they believe is better for one's health.

Rastas would not change anything about themselves. They just hope that people will eventually accept them as they are. They themselves accept everyone else as they are, and yet society rejects them. But they are not intimidated by society's critique of their beliefs and lifestyle, although they know that the mouth is like a weapon that can go so far as to kill you. But for Rastas, the only part of the body that is pure is the heart. They don't want anyone to judge them by their appearance, but to speak with them and try and understand what it is they have in their minds.

The Rasta Mockers

There are many people – mainly male – who don't practise anything remotely Rastafarian, but imitate their physical appearance, like hair or dress styles. These males shave all their hair around the sides of their head and leave only some at the top. They knot the hair on the top, just like the locks of the Rastas. For certain Rastas, this is seen as a form of mockery. But for the true Rasta, each individual lives their life their own way – if they want to look like that, then why not? The true Rasta is only against the ex-Rastas, those who have cut their hair and given up everything about Rasta teachings, because they are afraid of what society thinks of them. Such would never discourage the true Rasta. They simply grow their hair to follow Jah's example but they say you don't have to dread your hair to be a Rasta, for 'being a Rasta comes from the heart.' What upsets Rastas is when their fellow Rastas change overnight because Rastafarianism teaches how to be oblivious to society's many temptations, and just be yourself ('I and I', as they say).

Alcohol and Rastas

A true Rasta will never drink to the point that he's drunk and go on the streets, harass others, and take what is not theirs. They are really not a threat to society. They don't use substances that Haile Selassie doesn't use. Whoever uses other substances or drugs apart from the healing herb (marijuana) are disrespecting Selassie's law. The Rastas will take chemical medication, but they believe it's better to use the plant, because Jah provides them with these in abundance to use and each plant has its purpose. One only has to believe in the healing power of the plant. If you are ill, and taking the herb doesn't make you better, then you can turn to chemical products. Jah gives us everything we need, like medicinal plants; but Babylon doesn't give the people the knowledge on how to utilise this plant to its full potential. Today there are many people who are ill, and still there is no medication in pharmacies to help.

We need to remember that nature contains all the good things people need. Modern Western medicine, even while knowing very little about marijuana, preaches to people about its harmful side effects. But Rastas wait for the help of the government, to educate the nation on the truth about this plant, not what laboratories have concluded. The Rasta dream is to legalise marijuana. The question for them is, why is marijuana illegal while alcohol is legal? Each day they ask themselves the same question. How many people have lost their lives on the road because of alcohol? On the other side, how many people lose their lives because of marijuana? Until now, they haven't gotten any responses, because this has never happened. When someone has had an accident and has used both marijuana and alcohol, the government claims that the cause of the accident was the marijuana. Rastas would like to see all this misconception, this propaganda, about marijuana end.

The other question for them concerns tobacco and cigarettes. Why does the government legalise cigarettes? While at the same time it tells people that it is dangerous for your health. Cigarettes and alcohol are dangerous, and yet legal. Why is it that marijuana is placed in the same category and yet is illegal? This is dangerous for your health, they say, and purchase it at your own risk. To Rastas, this clearly means that governments do not care about the people. The question Rastas would like to put forth to the governments: what sort of message is this law communicating to its people? What the Rastas would like is for cigarettes and alcohol to be prohibited just like marijuana, to be sure that the government exists to protect its people and not just its own financial interests.

A Look at Rastas in Jamaica

For the Jamaicans, reggae music is very culturally significant. The generation of Marleys, including Peter Tosh, Israel Vibration, LKJ, Burning Spear, Justin Hinds, Stranger Cole, and others will never be forgotten. Now the generation after Marley's takes reggae music even further, as they create various different styles but still stick to the reggae roofs. In Jamaica today, most people appreciate 'reggae ragga'. This is mainly used at the dance hall. Today, these reggae ragga artists influence the youths of Jamaica. At the very beginning of the rise in new styles of music, most of the lyrics spoke of luxury, money, guns, big cars, girls and sex. The youth of Jamaica were really influenced by these artists' ideologies, and after a certain time, their goals and values in life changed to reflect these materialistic ideas. In today's society, almost everyone wishes to achieve such materialistic goals. At the same time, they live alongside the Rastas, who have always sung about love, peace, togetherness and freedom. But for young people of today, that's not enough and they prefer to listen to their idols, who are part of modern society. Some violence in Jamaica is caused by such youths. Some of reggae ragga music was banned from the radio because many of the lyrics spoke of violence or racism. After a while, most of these artists realised that it doesn't make sense to create music which transmitted such messages, which gets banned by radio stations; it is they who are the losers in the end.

The Jamaican youths believe that Rastas suffer from mental slavery. For them, the past is the past, and we should live in the present. They would like the Rastas to remember the following line from one of Bob Marley's songs: 'Emancipate yourself from mental slavery, none but ourselves can free our minds.' Until the Rastas do this, they will not be able to appreciate living in Jamaica. For the Rastas believe that everyone has a goal in them, and this goal is to return to their land, the Promised Land – Africa. The day they reach their promised land, Jamaicans will finally feel at home, because to feel at home, one has to be in one's homeland. Since slavery, when they were taken away from Africa, they have never been able to return. Every day the white races claim that Jamaicans are originally from Africa, but if they are, what are they doing in Jamaica? When all this history is cleared perhaps they can finally feel at home in Jamaica. Rastas dream not only of seeing blacks coming together, but also for all blacks to be united. They don't really think that blacks should only stick with blacks, but that each colour can be mixed – just don't forget who you are.

The Life of Rastas

Most Jamaican Rastas live in the mountains or hills. They are nearly all farmers. They grow vegetables to be sold in the market, and in their spare time, they make clothes to sell, so that they can have a little extra money, just enough to help them pay their bills. Each Friday or Saturday, they will take their vegetables to the market. They may have a wooden cart in which they put their vegetables on for sale. Most of these vegetables are calalloo, cabbage, lettuce and cucumber. It's not very easy for them to be in town because of certain people who will stare at them, criticise them or simply be too scared to go near them. They are only there to sell their vegetables, long enough to earn a little money.

Sometimes, they will have been in the market for many hours and still not have sold any of their vegetables. They will then try to draw the attention of potential customers by singing the time 'People, people, Selassie son selling', or 'I and I have all types of vegetables selling, like calalloo and cabbage, lettuce and cucumber!' Some people will buy from them out of pity or because of the manner in which they publicise themselves.

After they have sold their vegetables, they will go do their own shopping for some essentials they cannot produce themselves. After that, they will return home to their houses in the mountain. That's the only way they can feel at home – with their wife and children; together, they are one big happy family, in unity and love, far away from aggressive people. The Rastas are not lazy; they work six days a week on their farm. They produce things that nature provides them with. They are not just vegetarians, but eat food free of salt, preservatives and additives. They avoid too much coffee, alcohol or other drugs.

The Rasta's Children's Education

Living in society is not very easy for Rastas and their children. Every day they live a double lifestyle; one at home and another at school. But they accept this existence because they know it's necessary; as they have heard their fathers say: it is the 'Babylon system'. What children learn at school, and what they learn from their parents are two different things. But again, as their fathers say: 'We chose sense out of nonsense.' That is to say, Rastas know what is right and what is wrong. But they also know that to express themselves in public would cause conflict so they always keep their last words to themselves. They are taught by their parents to be respectful and this they display in their everyday lifestyles. And yet, at school, because of their appearance, they are first to be noticed by the teachers, who always ask them questions, as if they were the only ones in class.

It's also very difficult for Rastas children to make friends at school because of the way they think. They are often mocked for their ideas and lifestyle. Sometimes when they stand in lines at school, there's always someone who will pick on them, or tease them to make others laugh. But for the Rastas, 'He who laughs last laughs best.' But in spite of this they retain their long clumpy hair, as Jah did, and gain morale knowing that it was not very easy for Jah either to live in society. With faith, the Rastas know the truth: that each one of us lives what he learns. Have faith in Jah Rastafari, Selassie I, the first king of kings, lord of lords, the conquering lion of the tribe of Judah, as the Rastas say. As the Rastas accept others, they would like others to accept them. They say, give your heart to Jah, and everything will follow; he will show you the way to love. Everyone who calls on Jah's name will be blessed, because Jah has created him or her for his glory, and he's here to help him or her.

The Women Rastas

The women Rastas in Jamaica are mainly the wives of the male Rastas. These women work on their husbands' farms or as vendors in markets. They sell things that they make themselves. They learn how to make clothes by embroidering, after which they learn to make hats, belts and clothes for babies.

Their husbands will go to the mountain to pick a type of fibre called wicker. These plants are then sun-dried and used to make furniture, which they sell in villages and towns. These people are very creative and they make marvellous things by hand. After they sell their crafts, they come out with more of an idea on the needs of their customers, and will prepare this for the market the week after.

These Rasta women are also excellent mothers, and spend a lot of time educating their children. There are certain Rastas who wish that they had their own schools for their children. They know what they teach their children won't fall on deaf ears, but on fertile ground, which will bring forth good fruits one day.

The Other Side of Rastas

The Rastas don't find it difficult to mix with non-Rastas. They don't even try to force others to think like them. But they know that in Jamaican society it can be very, very difficult for them to integrate into almost all workplaces, because of their particular way of dressing, eating and expressing themselves. For example, to work in the police force or at a bank, they have to have short hair or dress in suits or uniforms. Some people would find it shocking to see a Rasta work in these kinds of environments. But a Rasta's ambition is not really grounded in this sort of work or trying to establish a career. What they really want is to educate the Jamaicans about their culture, and it is reward enough for them to catch the attention of some Jamaicans who take an interest in the truth about their 'hidden' history. The Rastas will never change anything about themselves. They believe that until they are accepted and recognised by everyone, people will simply have to deal with their parallel existence.

The Lives of Rastas in Towns

There are certain Rastas willing to prove to non-Rastas that they are able to lead a 'normal' life in towns. They will function in the normal world, according to society's rules and moves, but they will also try as much as possible to keep their own traditions while doing so.

These Rastas tend to be their own bosses and run record shops or clothes stores. Those who own stores will show to others that even if they sell modern clothing, they still retain their own sense of dress. They live in hope that people will eventually see and accept them as they are, in spite of their difference, just as they accept everyone with their differences. Sometimes the Rastas are treated badly by others, and thought of as 'lazy' or 'dirty'. Most Rastas will never bother going into an employment agency to get work. They know it is just a waste of time, because they know that they will immediately be judged by their appearance. Those Rastas who can't afford to be their own boss tend to become farmers.

The Ital Party

The ital party is a party where Rastas celebrate at their homes with others. They will invite others, including non-Rastas (everyone is welcome), to share their food and will prepare their favourite dishes, most of which are a mixture of fish and vegetables. They prepare lots of naturally made juice, because they consume little or no alcohol. All these dishes are without salt, which is why it is called 'ital'. At these parties, they will mostly listen to reggae music, or play guitars and drums. They will talk about Jah's love, which is symbolised by the fact that everyone is together, with no hatred in the heart, just love, like it could be paradise on earth. They will roll a 'spliff', a mixture of marijuana and tobacco, which they pass around for everyone to take a 'draw'. They will never force anyone to smoke, if they don't want to. While smoking, they have to look out for the police as parties like these tend to attract unwanted attention from the local authorities. If they were to be caught smoking cannabis, there is a high probability of spending the night in prison, or having to pay a fine. The police are often called 'Babylon' as they represent the injustices and prejudices that society bears upon them. Simply when passing by the police station, they may be called in and searched for marijuana. The police know that they aren't criminals, but only that they use an illegal drug.

The True Living God

The Rastas have strong faith and believe that Haile Selassie is the true god who Marcus Garvey prophesied as such. He is thought to have said, 'Look in Africa; a black king will be crowned. Haile Selassie was crowned king in Ethiopia.' The Rastas believe in the bible, but they think that certain Christians did not correctly interpret certain scriptures. They are not against Christianity or any religion, but what they are against is what is taught to the people. They have a different understanding of the word 'paradise'; they believe that paradise is here on earth, that if everyone came together, prayed together, and shared their joy, heaven would be here on earth. Rastas are still waiting to see their paradise, which is since the time when their tribe in Israel was separated and taken from Africa to be sold as slaves to return to Africa. When they finally reach this 'promised land' and their tribes reunite, they will feel like they are in paradise. All their troubles will be over and they will finally feel at home, where everyone unites in love and all hatred will be finished once and for all. They would listen to their reggae music, have good times, give praises to Jah, and rejoice in knowing that they are far away from the 'Babylon system'. They know that this will take many years, but they don't lose faith. The next half of history will be told the day they return to Africa.

The Grand Market in Jamaica

The grand market is celebrated each December, the day before Christmas. This market lasts for about twenty-four hours. Everyone will go in the town that is nearest to them. Brown's Town is grand market's capital, and nearly everyone who lives in small villages goes to Brown's Town. The market starts at about 3 a.m. and it is where many people buy their Christmas things. At about three or four in the afternoon, the prices drop. These vendors know that during the night there are too many people, and nearly everyone is there to eat and dance. There are usually many big sound systems set up on the road, and as the music is played very loud, it's almost impossible to hear when someone speaks.

In the afternoon some people will wear colourful costumes; they are generally known as 'muscuray'. They scare passers-by by their manner. This is an old past of Jamaican tradition, which is definitely disappearing and little or nothing is now known about it. As these people enjoy the results of their pranks, the Rastas will remark, 'Dem belly full but dem starving,' which is to say their stomachs are full but they don't know what tomorrow might bring. As the Rastas listen to their music, they will raise their lighters in the air and say, 'Let Jah be praised, while I pray for my blessing to arrive.'

Certain Rastas will not have been into town for eleven months. Only at Christmas, they will leave the hills. Rastas tend to live on a hill in East Jamaica called 'Orange hill' or 'Heggins hill'. They prefer to live in the east because of a proverb which says, 'Even when they are in their graves, they'll always be depressed, there's no life in the West, because the East is the best.' They believe that if they were to live in the west of Jamaica, they would always have bad dreams and hence feel depressed.

The Discovery of Jamaica

The Rastas believe that the history of Columbus' discovery of the Americas is false. They believe that Columbus never discovered Jamaica. How could he 'discover' Jamaica, when the Arawaks were originally there? They believe that if Columbus had never been to Jamaica, the Arawak Indians would still exist today. 'Christo-their come robbed us.' They will never forgive this man who pretended to be friendly with the natives but gave orders at the same time to destroy them. Though they say a plant known as Casava killed the Arawaks, the Rastas know better. Columbus made people think that there, finding food to eat was difficult and not even wild animals could be found in the mountains, and the only thing the natives were able to find were cassava – that because they ate this plant before it was ripe, they were poisoned. For the Rastas, this is just falsified history. They know that someone killed the Arawaks. It seems that Jamaican history, true Jamaican history, has been forgotten. The only people who won't forget are the Rastas, and they maintain the custom of naming their businesses after the Arawaks.

The Deliverance

Today, Jamaica has some of the most talented Rasta musicians in the world. These include: Buju Banton, Beenie Man, Capleton, Ninja Man, Sizzla and Anthony B, just to name a few. They transmit the Rasta message through their songs. By listening to their lyrics, you know exactly who they are. These artists don't like it when people call them rich, because for them, being rich should not mean having a lot of money, but having lots of knowledge and being wise and passing on this wisdom to others through music. People overseas think of them as celebrities, but in Jamaica they don't live the lives of celebrities, but the life of a humble man, one who works honestly for his bread. Sometimes, listening to their music, you can understand that they don't make music just for people to purchase and consume, but to listen to and take it in as food for their spirit. Each day in their prayers, these Rasta musicians ask Jah for guidance, because they know life is difficult. They always ask this question: 'Do true Rastas exist?' And they ask Jah to deliver them from sins, to let them be clean before his eyes, and let them be here to help people who are in need. As say the Rastas, 'The ancient days are over, we are now living in the present.' As they pray together, 'Bless me, Jah Rastafari, because no one is perfect in your eyes.' As they come together to worship, they say, 'Help us, oh Jah because we feel that deliverance is near.'

Society's Pleasure

Today it's not only the Rastas who are disrespected by certain people in society, but also all those whom society considers abnormal. To be normal in this society, one has to do exactly what average people do. In this society, the word abnormal is used each second of the day. Society does not accept someone trying to be different from others, by their mode of dress, their eating habits or by their beliefs. When one does something that is different from others one is considered to be abnormal or deviating from the norm. If one refuses to follow society's temptations, by wearing the latest fashions, one is thought to be old-fashioned or un-modern. For Rastas, this is a form of racism. In certain circumstances it's the society that chooses how you should live your life, by telling you what to wear, how to do things and what to say. If one doesn't obey thee rules, one is perceived to be disrespectful or irresponsible. There is always someone to judge one by one's appearance, but never to judge one by what one has in the heart. Rastas will not let anyone change them or rearrange them, because it's *their* life, and they have only that one life to live. They would like people to realise that while they are pointing their fingers at others, somebody else is pointing at them. For them, what is most important is love, to be yourself and accept others no matter who they are. Don't judge others by their appearance or their skin colour; each one has a message to give. It takes everyone with all these differences to make society. Educate the children, teach them love and respect and they'll learn to accept and respect others.

Christianity, the Religion Practised by Most Jamaicans

At least one person out of each Jamaican family goes to church. Jamaica is a Christian country where nearly everyone believes in God. Most Jamaicans go to church on Saturdays or Sundays. They refer to the bible: 'Remember the Sabbath, to keep it holy.' Those who worship on Saturdays believe that you shouldn't do certain things during the rest of the week: play music that isn't Christian, for example, or even do some shopping. On Sundays, nearly every house is quiet. If someone were to pass on the street, all that they would hear would be music playing – Christian music. The very faithful will wake up extremely early in the morning to prepare their dinners for after church.

For the Rastas, the practice of going to church on Saturdays or Sundays, as do the Christians, is just like remembering God (Jah) only on these particular days. They believe that this way of worshipping is mistaken. Rastas don't believe in the offering for they think, 'How can you help others by just believing in God? They believe that the preachers have many opportunities to educate their congregations, as they believe that he's a true man of God.

For the Rastas to merely get some attention from these people is not enough. Their aims are to unite the people and make them come together to worship Jah in the way they were taught he should be praised. They believe in the Bible to be the 'true book' and that it will protect them from their enemies. Most of the time they keep the Bible on them – to have Jah and his word with them at all times.

The Sunsplash in Jamaica

The Sunsplash is the biggest reggae festival in Jamaica. Artists come from home and abroad to enjoy five days of music. To begin the concert, they always have an artist of the same generation as Bob Marley plan an opening tune – like Burning Spear. The young reggae ragga artists have a lot of respect for these older reggae artists. Each night of this festival is unforgettable, as different artists perform. For the Jamaicans who are great fans of these artists it's a chance to see some of the most well-known names of the reggae world perform: Shaggy, Beenie Man, Bounty Killer, Buju Banton among others. As these artists perform, the women go wild and shout, take off their clothes and try as much as possible to be closest to the stage so that they don't miss anything. Some of the women are so fanatical that they become jealous of these artists as though they were their husbands. When they sing their songs, the lyrics make some women sad. Singer song-writer Buju Banton sang, 'Love me car, love me bike, live me money and things but most of all me love me browning.' Just hearing these lyrics make some women sad. They would like to try to let Buju know that when they hear this song they are really unhappy. And Buju will try as much as possible to sing lyrics that these women love. But he did the opposite by saying, 'Buju no stop cry all black woman, respect all the women with dark complexion.' So I guess Buju was in some ways a bit of a comedian.

Most of these artists come from the ghettos in urban areas. The only way they can express themselves is through their music, as does the singer Bounty when he talks about life in the ghetto in many of his lyrics. He would like others to know that when one wakes up every day having nothing to do, all that passes through one's mind is to pick up a gun. These artists who make songs about the ghetto life do so because they know what it is like. Listening to their lyrics is like listening to a poem, a message for the nation. These lyrics make you think twice.

The African Pride

Rastas believe strongly in fighting for their rights, but to obtain this, they will not tolerate any shedding of blood. This fight requires much patience, but no brutality, in order for black nations to move forward. They asked themselves the question over and over: 'Why can't we be united?' All that needs to be done is to put all our differences aside; we must come together, cease war and fighting. As they say, 'Who knows better must do better.' They believe that since slavery the black population was made unhappy and told many lies. But now the black people are allowed education, they now have the opportunity to learn right from wrong. They thank Jah for the knowledge of musical communication, because this helps them to come together, because togetherness is what the black nations need.

When they think of Africa, they say, 'Africa, I'm crying over you, you know that's not the way it's supposed to be!' For them, it seems like Africa is rejected by some people because its riches were taken away and left only with the image of a country with many dangerous diseases and poverty. Rastas believe that when they return to Africa, everyone will unite and things will be much better, because together they will defend what's theirs. As say the Rastas, 'The rich are wise in this concept, but the poor are filled with understanding.'

The Rasta Lovers

The Rastas believe in love. When they love someone they will give them all their heart. When they think of the word 'love', for them, it's an unconditional feeling. They think that when someone is in love, his mind is at rest, and he wants to do his best. Being in love, you can never be the same; your face is pure delight –it's like you have all the love that you never had before. They believe love can never die or leave you; if someone loves you he/she will always love you, no matter the separation – you'll always linger in his/her heart. They believe: 'Take a women, and call her your wife.' This doesn't mean that they don't believe in being married, but they believe that one need not be married to have a solid relationship, if it is based on love. As the Rastas say, 'You never miss the water until the well runs dry.' Which is to say, while you are with someone, you get so used to this person that you don't know or remember what it means to be alone and so you think you need more space. Until this person is gone, you don't understand that you will only be left with an empty space and not personal space. When someone feels like his or her partners have rejected him, he/she feels unwanted, and ends up chasing after every beautiful man/woman in the street to compensate, which in the end, only serves to bring unhappiness into the home. For Rastas, when you love someone, questions of age, race, or colour do not matter. All that is important is to feel safe in your partner's arms, just like a baby.

Girls and Pets

As said before, there are certain reggae singers who make Jamaican women go wild. Their lyrics make women feel their love, as though they were close by. Most Jamaican girls' wishes are to spend one night with these artists, to know whether they are as romantic as the songs they sing. Shaggy and Buju Banton are said to be the most romantic of these artists and certain women will even break up with their partners because they can't make their love be felt the way these artists tell the women how it's supposed to feel. Certain Jamaican women even call their partners by these artists' names, and this make them feel ridiculous. These artists make women out to be the most beautiful things on earth, and that they need to be cherished the way a child cherishes his pets. For them, this world is neither for women nor men, but *our* world, and Jah created women for men. The Jamaican men like these artists; they are their idols.

The Jamaican Lifestyle

Many people compare the Jamaican lifestyle with that of Africa. From my experience, Jamaican lifestyle is far from that in Africa. Jamaicans know nothing of Africa and the only information they have is from the television. Jamaicans don't travel a lot – only when they have families in other countries – but they know that life in Jamaica is far from that in Africa. Jamaica is a poor country, but no one dies of famine, no one has gone hungry for many days, no one has a lack of shelter. Of course, there are exceptions – some lazy people who refuse to work honestly for their bread, or depend on society to provide their daily needs, or live by robbing others. In Africa today, many people suffer from famine, homelessness and disease.

Where education is concerned, it seems many African nations lack in a standard system. In Jamaica, everyone has the right to education; from ages six to fifteen, good schools are available to all. Sometimes they may be short of materials, because the schools are public and free, and the government funds everything. Everyone has an environment that's clean and hygienic. In Africa, most people's lives are far from being like that. Where health is concerned, Jamaican hospitals are equipped with nearly al the materials necessary. There are no serious contagious diseases in Jamaica, from which there is no protection, because the vaccinations are free.

As the Rastas say, 'No one knows what tomorrow might bring.' After many years of thinking, these Rastas came to the conclusion that it does not matter what your religion is, or what you eat or drink or what you say defines you, but what comes from the heart. The heart is the most wonderful part of the body. All the right decisions come from the heart. When the mind goes wrong in making a decision, let the heart take over, and you will never have any regrets.

Single Parent Life

Most Rastas are born of single-parent families. When they consider how hard their parent had to work to assume responsibility over them it makes their love grow stronger. Most times it's the mother who is responsible for them. They know that their mother had to play the role of both mom and dad. Sometimes they want their mother to know that when she cries, they are crying too, because when they see the look on her face, they are really sad. They encourage their mothers and comfort her, saying that even if her lover is gone, they are here for her more than ever. Rasta musicians have much respect for their mother and they will sometimes write their favourite songs for their mothers.

The Alpha Boys' School in Jamaica

The Alpha Boys' School is an institution that helps parents who have problems with their children, when they refuse to obey or integrate into society. Most of the artists of the eighties went to this institution. This school prepares them for careers in music, dance or other work that they prefer to do. Each person that goes to this school comes out with a career. The people who run this school are Roman Catholics, and most of the teachers are nuns. These women have a lot of love for the teenagers in their care, and they are always there to listen to them when they have a problem. The teenagers will form their own bands and create their own styles of music. Alpha is a learning and living institution. When the teachers think that these boys have learnt enough so that they can now live within their communities, they can leave the institution to start a career. These teachers open lots of windows of opportunity in the music industries for these boys, and they go on music tours to perform on stage in public. Sometimes the producers hear their music and like it immediately, in which case their career starts there.

This school still exists, in Kingston, Jamaica. This school for runaway children is a message to teenagers that no what matter their problem, there's always someone there to listen even if their parents can't understand or cope with them. Sometimes there are teenagers who would like to go there because Alpha is known for its excellent music tuition, but it's just a school for 'problematic' children. This school also teaches teenagers to use musical instruments. One can never be bored because there is always something to do. In Jamaica today there are many institutions like this, but not all specialise in music. Alpha is said to be the best because they teach you a trade, a vocation.

Although Jamaica is known as reggae country, Jamaicans are able to create other types of music, such as calypso and tango. Each year in Jamaica, they have a calypso competition; it's amazing how Jamaicans are talents at dancing the calypso. In the eighties, calypso and reggae were the only music that triggered the Jamaicans to dance. Today, music is part of the Jamican life; just to listen to music makes them happy. As the Jamaicans say, 'Life without music is miserable.' There are many big sound systems in Jamaica, such as Base Odyssey, Kilimanjaro, Stone Love, Metromedia among others. These sound systems are for rent. Most Jamaicans love these sound systems as they are considered to be the best on the island. The Jamaicans love it when the music is played very loud. The DJs know this, and they play the music that the people like.

Some Jamaicans will organise a big party at home and rent out the sound system for a night. This is not just an all-friend party but what is called a 'session'. This 'session' is a public party, and the hosts transform their houses into a bar, restaurant, and dance hall. It's very expensive to rent a sound system, but definitely worth it!

Our Heroes

Many Jamaicans consider Bob Marley a hero. They even compare him to an apostle or saint. Like Saint Peter, Marley spread the work of Jah to all our corners of the earth. Yet it wasn't very easy for him to capture the attention of the people, by preaching Jah's love for them. He was very smart, as he found a way to do this – by singing. Many people around the globe adored him and appreciated his songs, but there were some people who didn't like his image. But Marley was very proud to be a Rasta. He was sent by Jah to be the first Jamaican Rasta to represent his fellow Rastas. His death left many Rastas mourning. Today, he still lives in hearts of many Rastas. The Rastas have strong faith and now they do what Marley did – fight for their freedom, hoping that one day they'll be free. There is also Marcus Garvey, for Jamaicans he is more than a hero. He not only stood for his rights but for his culture, his people and his God. He taught the nation about his unjust life, and Rastas vow never to vouch for the same treatment. For Rastas, he's the most important person in their history, as he was the only one to tell them who they are really, and he founded the United Negro improvement association and accomplished many wonderful things in aid of the poorer black nations. With all his experience he knew that the only place that his people would be free was in their homeland.

Gargamels

Gargamels are men who can't help thinking of women, and find every woman attractive and irresistible. Certain men believe that they have been like this since birth. They think that it's like an illness, but for which there is no cure. Sometimes just listening to these women speak, makes their knees start trembling and their heart beats faster – just a weakness that has no cure.

Certain men provoke these feelings, just to prove to women that they are the most romantic men on earth, and they were created especially for them. Some of these men who are always 'eye-raping' women, have so many ideas in their minds, that even if they had all the women in the world they would still not be satisfied. For them, it is not a form of disrespecting women – always giving them compliments about their appearances – but comes from the heart.

Most Gargamels are single, as many Jamaicans who are married are faithful to their wives. Even if they have another woman in secret, they are not considered to be Gargamels. Certain DJs influence men to be Gargamels by making songs about how it feels to have more than one partner at a time. They tell these single people about their lives, how they had lots of women. When men who are single hear this, they want to experience it. But the Rastas ask, 'Where is love in these types of relationships?' They will never have this type of relationship. Although they realise that in today's world, especially in certain parts of Africa, this type of life is considered 'normal' – but where men can have all the women they wish. But that's the reason why life is so hard for them and that there are so many types of diseases. Rastas believe the human has one life and one god; live it right, in the way that Jah wished his people to live. They don't believe that some men are born like the Gargamels claim they are – for them no one is born like this. A person lives what he has learnt, and society has something to do with this.

43

Misty Days

Misty days', so called by the Rastas, are those days when there is misery, unhappiness, sickness, death and pain for them, Jamaica (Jam-Down), is a tropical climate and therefore everyone should keep their faces bright... and still, there are people who complain that they are too hot or that it's too windy. These people do not know the luck they have. But Rastas are sure that one day, these 'misty days' will be over. They know that there are times when people feel 'blue', but their hope is that paradise will be here on earth one day. Rastas believe that human beings are the hardest animals to please on earth. They know that until Jah purifies his people, cleanses their unclean hands, creates in them all a clean heart, life will be difficult for some people. They say that some people, even if they had everything they wished for, would still be unhappy, because it's their soul that is unhappy. They are waiting for the misty days to be over, and will never lose their confidence, as their ancestors never lost hope in their emancipation; they are here to let their ancestors know that their tears were not in vain, because they have received the second emancipation and they are waiting for the last, when they'll finally reach the land they were taken from. All of these bad times will always be remembered, but they would just be bad remembrances. So they tell their people, 'be strong', hold a firm meditation – one day, things will be better, just ask Jah for a guiding angel to watch over you, and his guidance and presence to protect you from evil thought and be patient; one day, like the start of a story – "once upon a time" – things will get better.'

'Girls Dem Phat!'

The Jamaican men like it when their women are really in shape, and being in shape, for these men, is not to be too fat or too slim. Certain singers gently mock women when they get too fat, and at the same time they will tell them not to worry, because there are many slim women who are jealous of them. There are many Jamaican men who like it when their women are fat – because these women protect them and keep them warm – they don't like women who are too slim, because they can have many health problems, even when carrying a baby.

What Rastas say to all these problems – too slim, too fat, too small or too tall – is, 'Who are we to judge someone by their appearance? Jah creates his people in his own image.' They also believe that they are not the only ones to be criticised by their appearance, but everyone that society considers to be 'different'. They aren't afraid of what society thinks of them because even those who think that they are better than others are far from being perfect, because we are all imperfect.

Today, certain human beings try to go against the will of Jah, by trying to create a human statue; but they cannot give life to this statue – no one goes before God. The Rastas tell people who suffer all types of racism 'Just be yourself, never change anything of yourself for the love of someone, but only for the love of oneself. They know that in this society, if you are not strong, you can easily break down. In times like these, just leave everything to Jah – he'll find a solution.

'Gal'

The word 'gal' (girl) is used by many Jamaican signers and DJs in the dance hall. Certain women go wild when these DJs call women by this term, as they find this really romantic. The DJs are very proud to tell women that they have many 'gal' friends. They are really actors, as they pretend to each woman that she is the most beautiful in their eyes.

The Herb

The Rastas say 'Jah give us the herb for the service of mankind.' They have found this 'service' and they include the herb in everything they use and smoke it.

Studio One

Studio One is without doubt the most important record label in the history of Jamaican music. It is in many ways the foundation label of reggae music. It has led the way throughout the evolution of reggae music in Jamaica. From the very first ska records, through rock steady, roots DJs and dubplates, Studio One has produced music of very high quality throughout its reign. Its rhythms are as popular as they were thirty years ago, as singers and producers of Jamaica reuses and re-records them to make new songs. They most talented Jamaican artists started their careers with Studio One – namely, burning Spear, Freddy MacGregor, Marcia Griffiths, Bob Marley, Lee Perry, just to name a few. Today in Jamaica, as things and times change, many Jamaican artists have their own recording studios at home, but Studio One will never be forgotten, because it's always produced the best sounds.

Give Thanks

'Let Jah be praised, while I and I pray for my blessings to arrive,' the Rastas say. They believe in giving Jah thanks for each day because no one knows what tomorrow might bring – they know what yesterday was like, and they have seen today, but tomorrow, only Jah knows. The Rastas make only short-term plans; they have dreams and wishes, but they would never make plans for the next ten years.

Backbiters

The 'backbiters', so called by the Rastas, are those people who pretend as though they are with you, but behind your back, think nothing of you. Even though Rastas are always on good terms with everyone, and stay amongst themselves in the mountains, minding their own business, there are always some people who will bad-mouth them, just because they are Rasta.

Skylarkers

'Skylarkers' are those who refuse to work, or pretend that there are no jobs for them because they do not have any qualifications. These persons stay on the road nearly nine hours a day, as if they were working to earn their wages. The Rastas believe that if these people don't do something about this, they will live under these circumstances all their lives. They believe that these people are prone to commit criminal acts, as they want many things but because they do not work and find it very difficult to be honest, they start robbing to get 'quick money'. At the same time, they think that it is the parents who are at fault for spoiling their children and giving them everything they wish. After a while as teenagers, the children find that working is too difficult, or that they don't want to work for minimum wages. Some Skylarkers watch people as they do their shopping and ask for a ten-cent or a five-cent coin, but this cannot help. In society today, this is a really big problem, because even very young children have begun doing this. There also exists what are called independent Skylarkers – those who write on a piece of paper, asking for some money. They sit beside this piece of paper, sometimes with their dogs. They don't harass anyone, and it's your choice to give them money or not.

But there are those who don't have the choice; begging is the only way they have of getting some money, other than borrowing. There are even those who can't work because of a handicap. Rastas consider that, for those people who are in these situations, begging is a necessity, but those who do this out of pure laziness must stop it before it's too late and they get out of order.

'Bal' Heads'

The bal' heads are people who consider themselves 'normal', who think that women should grow their hair, and that men should have short hair. Most of them are prejudiced against Rastas, as they not only grow their hair long but also knot it, and practice the religion of Rastafarianism. The Rastas know that these people do not accept them, but they are not even against this kind of biased thinking. Some of these people consider Rastas a danger to society in spite of never having talked to them. The Rastas know that they are not a danger to society, as they have never caused any kind of disruption whatsoever. They know that they are the ones who respect the environment the most. They never do anything to harm anyone; all they do is respect others just like they would like to be respected themselves. They believe that each time someone suffers, it is because of the bal' heads.

Positive Vibes

To have positive vibes is to always be on good terms, and be in a happy mood. The Rastas believe that you don't need lots of money to be happy, but to be with someone that you really love – this is what brings happiness. They think that some people, especially the working class, are too stressed because they allow no time for relaxation after a very hard day. When someone has eight hours' sleep, it's good for the body, but one doesn't really have to get eight hours sleep to be ready for the next day – a few hours is sufficient. They also believe that most people don't know how to rest, and this is the reason why some people, even while getting eight hours' sleep, wake up in the morning with tired eyes. They also believe in relaxation, as a sport, which helps people to look younger. They think that this is another reason for them to live in the mountains; because in towns, life is too speedy, and even when you are at home, there's too much noise, and people find it difficult to concentrate on themselves. They think that if someone really wants to feel well, they have to live in the mountains, where there is nothing to disturb them. If someone knows how to relax, they will always be on form. Rastas tell people how to relax – tell them to close their eyes; to try not to think of anything and forget tomorrow's activities; and if they can't help thinking about something that weights on their minds, then to think of a song, the song they love best – which helps to relax and prepare the spirit for tomorrow.

'Jam Down'

Jamaica is called 'Jam Down' by the Rastas because of its musical vibes. For the Jamaicans, Jamaica is the best country on earth. For the Rastas, the best country is Africa, as they don't consider Jamaica to be their land. Most of them stay in Jamaica because they don't have a choice for the moment. When the right time comes, they will find their promised land. They have nothing against Jamaica, but they say that it is not where their ancestors were taken from and therefore cannot feel at home there.

The End of Time

Many Rastas believe that this world will never end; according to the Bible, 'The world is without end.' They believe that the end of the world is when someone has died – only Jah alone knows what will happen after. They don't believe in heaven for certain people, and hell for others, but they believe that one who does what Jah expects him to do will be rewarded. For those who don't' believe that there is a God, one day Jah will show them signs and wonders – God will soften the hearts of those whose hearts are tough, and when this happens heaven will be here on earth.

Printed in the United Kingdom
by Lightning Source UK Ltd.
110770UKS00001B/46-54